TRANSLATING
YOUR SUCCESS

TRANSLATING YOUR SUCCESS

The Student Guide to Transforming Your Small Wins Into Big Wins

Carlos J. Malave

ISBN-13: **9781544724706**
ISBN-10: **1544724705**
Library of Congress Control Number: 2017904610
CreateSpace Independent Publishing Platform
North Charleston, South Carolina

Table of Contents

Dedication

I dedicate this book to my parents, Eva Rosado & Carlos R. Malave, to my loving wife, Melissa Timothy, and to my beautiful daughter, Thais Eva Malave.

Growing up, my mother would always say "It doesn't matter if it's a book, magazine or a newspaper, find time, and READ IT." And time is exactly what she had us find. She had us reading after school, during weekends and even on school holiday breaks. She was big on education. As an elementary teacher, she pushed every one of her students and her own three children all the same. Education was her way out of poverty, and she believed it would keep us from mediocrity. Although I may have fought against most of her reading sessions and teaching procedures growing up, I am eternally grateful that she stuck with her methods and held her ground. She is the reason I got into the field of education, became a teacher, speaker, and now an author. This one is for you, Ma! I love you and thank you!

Working construction and always having side jobs on the weekends made my father the work horse of the family. He was the true provider and supporter to all our crazy dreams. He made sure we had everything we needed and wanted growing up. He assured us that if we worked hard for what we wanted, then we could have it. He would say "Nothing in this world is free, Papi. To get anything, you have to work for everything." When I was 18 years old, he took me to work construction with him for a summer and it was the hardest couple of months I have ever had working anywhere. But for the first time in my life, I got to see how hard my father works daily. I watched him wake up every morning at 4 a.m., drive an hour to work, bust his tail off on the job until 3:30 p.m., drive back home an hour, go to the gym to work out for another two hours, then go home, and do it all over again every day, for 3 months until I went off to college. He is the reason I work as hard as I do. Thank you for showing me the way, Pa! I love you!

Since we met in the summer of 2011 working for the local YMCA Summer Youth Camp in Ridgewood New York, my wife Melissa has been my best friend, my confidant, my advisor, and biggest supporter. She is the one who taught me how to dress, and how to love and care sincerely for others. My wife's sacrifices for our union and family has put me in the position that I am in today. She is the most genuine and considerate person I know and she has been nothing but a great influence in my life. Her way of dealing with people and problems goes unmatched. I've learned a great deal from her, and I plan to continue to learn from her and love her for the rest of my life. She is the reason I am the husband, father, son, and person people see today. With all my heart, I love you! Thank you, Melissa!

In 2014, I became a father to a beautiful little girl, and my role as a man and understanding of what a man is changed forever. I lead my life as an example for her now. She is watching my every move, and I want to represent a genuine perception of what a man is supposed to look like. Thais Eva Malave is my motivation, and the reason I stay on top of my duties and take my responsibilities as a man as serious as I do. I hope I make you proud when you read this one day! Love you, Thai!

And to the rest of my family:

"Hoy me presento ante ustedes un hombre que se a encontrado asi mismo. El cielo no es mi límite. Yo lo hice y no hay nada ni nadie que me pueda detener. Este es mi tiempo!! MI TIEMPO!"

TRANSLATION-

"I stand before you a man who has found himself. The sky is the limit from here. I did it and there is nothing or no one that can stop me now. This is my time! MY TIME!"

I love you all, Thank you.

Introduction: Making the Translation

I grew up in a bilingual household, where Spanish and English were the two primary languages used. My father spoke to us mostly in Spanish, while my mother would speak to us mostly in English. We would go back and forth so much within the day that we ended up creating what we called "Spanglish". As I began to learn the meanings to words in both Spanish and English, I quickly noticed that two words that meant the same thing didn't have to look the same way all the time. An example of this would be the two words- "Adios" and "Goodbye". These two words are spelt differently and look nothing alike but mean the same thing. This caught my attention at the time but I had no clue how this would impact me later in life.

As I got older and more experienced with life, I saw that success appeared differently for me as it did for those around me. Early on, my biggest successes came from playing sports and making friends. However, in contrast, my siblings' big successes early on came from within the classroom. And to be honest, their successes were more valued than mine were to everyone around us. I wasn't seen as the one who would succeed. That really bothered me for some time. It led me to believe that maybe I couldn't do as well in the classroom as I did out on the basketball court or track. But then my sophomore year at college came around, and something clicked.

I remembered being younger and learning about how words in Spanish and English could have the same meanings, but they almost never had to look the same. That memory made me think about my successes verses my siblings' successes. It was then that I began to make the connection between the translation of words and the successful experiences of people. The success that I experienced and the success that my sibling's experienced both gave us all the same feeling of accomplishment; but our successes didn't have to look the same for us to feel that same sense of accomplishment. This thought blew my mind. And from that day forth, I made my TRANSLATION! I began to make the connections from my early successes to my future successes. Translating my success, transformed my mind, and changed my life!

My purpose in writing this book is to help people across the world make their connections and translate their early success into long-term success. In three, simple steps, I will lay out the blueprint to what helped me overcome my fears and led me to become the person I am today. Growing up, my father told me, "Don't just talk; walk the walk, and that's when people will listen." I wrote this book with that thought in mind. Along with every step, I will share an experience and life lesson that connects to each point and step in this book. I promise you there is something in here that you will connect or relate to. ENJOY the Read!

Step I: Becoming Consciously Fit

This step is about becoming aware of your surroundings and perceiving your experiences correctly so that you can lead a successful life.

1

Understanding His Pain

"A father is a man who expects his son to be as good a man as he meant to be."

FRANK A. CLARK
AMERICAN WRITER & CARTOONIST

My father drank alcohol a lot while I was growing up. I used to think that he was in control and that he could stop whenever he wanted to until this one night. I remember it like it was yesterday. It was a long, lonely night. I tried everything to stay up but somewhere along the line, I fell asleep. I had that dream, you know, the one where you start falling, for no reason. Yes, that dream. I woke up in the middle of the night in a cold sweat, worried and wondering if everything was ok. Something just didn't feel right. Then I heard some noise coming from outside my bedroom. Trying not to wake my younger brother up, I tiptoed to the door. I cracked open the door, and the light from the hallway bathroom hits my eye. As I walked closer, I noticed and heard that the shower was on. Now I started to bug out because no one takes showers at 3 in the morning at my house, and especially not in the guest bathroom. I pushed the door open, and I felt the steam from the room. Nervous, scared, and worried of what I would see, I gathered the courage and pulled the curtain open. I look down and see my father, fully clothed with a shirt, pants, and boots on, blacked out with the water hitting him in the face and him trying to wake himself up out of his drunken state. That was the first time I realized that ADDICTION was real. It was the first moment I noticed that ADDICITION had my father. I was 12.

For a long time, I was angry with my father. I hated when he drank. It infuriated me the way he would act before he went out to drink, when he was drinking, and how he would disappear when he was drunk. I told myself I would never be like my father. That anger I had for my father's drinking became my motivator. But as I got older, my consciousness began to grow. I became more aware of what was going on. I realized that maybe I was asking the wrong questions all along. I would always say "Pa, why won't you stop drinking? Just stop!". I never once asked "pa, why do you drink?"

You will only start to understand people better when you figure out why they do what they do. What are the reasons behind people's ways? That is the question. And this is the question that started my conversation with my father when I was home from college. And I learned that my father lost his father from drinking when he was 7 years old. My father was a witness to domestic violence his whole life. My father was physically and mentally abused as a child from family and friends. You see, my father kept that pain inside of him not knowing how to deal with it. Drinking made him forget all of it, made him feel free, drinking let him be. Learning all of this, changed me and my reasons. At first, anger motivated me to think that I would never be a drunk. Learning my father's story motivated me to believe that I could be a drunk if I wasn't in control.

There's a famous Jay-Z line that goes "Like I told you sell drugs; no, HOV' did that, so hopefully you won't have to go through that". That line made me think of my father, and every time that song came on the radio, I switched up the words to that line to say "My pops went through that so hopefully I wouldn't have to go through that". My father had his faults, and he wasn't perfect by any means, but his purpose was clear. He worked hard so that his children could live better lives than he did. I believe every generation is supposed to be better than the last. Our jobs are to make our last names greater than their past. But we won't make our lives better if we don't take time to understand the past. The first, and most important, step to take towards you translating your success into long- term success is to learn about people's reasons, and then find your reasons. Begin today! Ask the right questions and grow!

ACTION STEP I

Who is that person that you need to talk to? Write their name down.

_____

_____

_____

_____

_____

_____

_____

_____

_____

_____

What are the questions that you need to ask this person? Write them down. List 1-3 below.

_____

_____

_____

_____

_____

_____

_____

_____

_____

_____

Why are you asking? What are your reasons for knowing?

_____

_____

_____

_____

_____

_____

_____

_____

_____

How could learning this information benefit you?

_____

_____

_____

_____

_____

_____

_____

_____

_____

_____

Sit down with that person you need to talk to and ask him/her the questions you wrote down. How did the conversation go? What did you learn?

_____

_____

_____

_____

_____

_____

_____

_____

_____

In the next chapter, you will learn about the importance of self-belief and how you can develop the belief in yourself progressively.

2

Belief in Self

"Sometimes you've got to believe in someone else's belief in you until your belief kicks in."

LES BROWN
AMERICAN MOTIVATIONAL
SPEAKER & AUTHOR

My parents always told me I could be anything I wanted to be when I grew up, but for some reason, I didn't fully trust them. Even if my parents believed it, I felt that it was their job to tell me that I would be great; that's what parents do. It wasn't until I got to high school where that changed, and I started to develop faith in myself.

Once I turned 15 years old, I began to realize that my coaches, mentors, and school counselors were telling me the same things that my parents were telling me for years. My Coach Powell told me once "Carlos, you will be successful in life not because of who you are but rather how you work. Your effort will always transfer." Although I still had some doubt, I began to give in. I decided to start trusting in my coach's and parents' belief in me. So, I closed my eyes and took the leap.

I started with believing in my work ethic and how it could take me places I could only dream of. My Coach Powell believed that if I put in the same work and effort that I did on the basketball court into everything else I was involved in, then I could be anything I wanted to be. So, I tested it out. I started putting in the same effort that I did on the court into the classroom. And surprisingly, it worked! I remember all the late nights studying and preparing for the next test or class project and being extremely tired. There were countless times I was on the edge and ready to quit, but I didn't. When those moments came, I connected it to the games. It became the 4th quarter, the home stretch, the last lap. And to a true competitor, there's no quitting in those moments. Those moments are what you work for as athlete, as a competitor. You must finish. And so, I did.

That experience gave me the courage to apply intense effort to everything I did. From then on, I gave 110% of myself to my academics, sports, relationships, family, and careers. My mentality shifted to give my all to what I do and see what happens afterwards. I figured that I was either going to succeed or learn from the experience. There was no losing for me.

I started out doubting myself and then I took the leap of faith. I began believing in my coach's and parents' belief in me until the belief in myself kicked in. Allow your belief in yourself to kick in, then develop and grow it. The results from it may blow you away!

<u>ACTION STEP II</u>
List as many people that believe in you and or who think positively about you? Write their names down.

_____

_____

_____

_____

_____

_____

_____

_____

_____

_____

List positive things that these people have told you.

_____

_____

_____

_____

_____

_____

_____

_____

_____

_____

Name someone you believe in and why you believe in them.

_____
_____
_____
_____
_____
_____
_____
_____
_____
_____

What are you going to take the leap of faith on? (Choose one goal) What's your first action towards building the belief in you achieving that goal?

_____
_____
_____
_____
_____
_____
_____
_____
_____
_____

In the next chapter, you will learn about your fears, how are they developed and how they have possibly been holding you back from achieving.

3

The Young, Foolish Mind

"It is inevitable that many ideas of the young mind will later have to give way to the hard realities of life."

Felix Bloch
Swiss Born American Physicist

We are all born with the young, foolish mind. Unaware of fear, limits, and barriers, which hold us back in our older years. It is the learned behaviors from our experiences that slows us down. I see this more clearly now as a father. When I'm running around and playing with my daughter, I always try to get her off guard and scare her. I want to see what she's made of. She chases me as I run towards the room to shut off all the lights and hide behind the door. As she enters the room, she looks around to scan the premises and slowly searches for her prey. I wait as she walks around determined to find her punk daddy. Once she's completely away from the door, I shut it and then jump at her like, AHHHHHHHHH!!! The room goes silent. I feel her hands on my cheeks as she grabs my face, then she laughs, opens the door, and walks out. I shake my head in disbelief and laugh myself. I've tried to scare her several times, in different situations, in all different rooms (bedrooms, bathrooms, living room and even closets). I even scared myself sometimes trying to get her. Over time, I concluded that, my baby is a THUG and isn't afraid of ANYTHING! But you see, at the age of two, my daughter doesn't know what fear is. She doesn't know what it is to fear or why to fear it. We are all born this way. It is the energy and vibe that is around us from young that gives us fear in our experiences. Right now, to my daughter, daddy jumping out at her in the dark is fun playtime for her. Why is that? You may ask. This is because, at this point in my daughter's life, she has only experienced laughter with her father in the dark. Now, something might happen to her later that will develop a fear of the dark in her, but right now, the dark represents fun playtime. What we experience young is what we deal with when we are older.

What happened to you in your youth? What gave you the fear that you still hold on to? Ask yourself these questions and revisit your past. The best way to overcome fear is to recognize what happened to you, so that you can face it dead on to be able to later move on.

ACTION STEP III
What is your #1 fear?

_____

_____

_____

_____

_____

_____

_____

_____

_____

_____

What's the earliest memory of you having that fear?
(Take some time and really look back.)

_____

_____

_____

_____

_____

_____

_____

_____

_____

_____

What will you do to overcome that fear? List 2-3 things you will try to do with in the year to overcome this fear. Write your list below.

_____

_____

_____

_____

_____

_____

_____

_____

_____

_____

In the next chapter, you will learn about the importance of facing your fears and how you can overcome them.

4

Overcoming Fear

"He who has overcome his fears will truly be free."

ARISTOTLE
ANCIENT GREEK PHILOSOPHER

I became free when I became fearless. I remember six years ago, thinking about how I've made it thus far and all the obstacles I had to overcome to get here. It was the proudest, and most exciting, moment of my life at the time. At the same time, I also recall it being the scariest, and most frightening, moment I have ever experienced. What's the next step? How do I start? Where am, I going? Where will I end up? And most importantly, who am I? It was as if I had shown up to class, and a pop quiz was being given out that was worth 50% of my grade, and I had just flunked the previous one. The test of life was on, and I wasn't sure if I was prepared to answer **all** the questions. The doubt began to overwhelm me, but you see, the crazy thing that I've learned about life is that these feelings are experienced by each one of us. Even the most talented and skilled have experienced it before they succeeded at a task. Their fear is almost always misperceived for confidence. For me, it's like the game of basketball. When I walk up to a new court, there's that moment of doubt. I question my skill and ability as fear starts to creep in. Can I perform? Are they better than me? Will I make a fool of myself this time? But rather than give in to fear, I accept it. I stay. The lyrics from "Lose Yourself" by Eminem play in my head, "He's nervous but on the surface, he looks calm and ready." The fear goes on until I finally get out there and start to play. It's then I realize that it's not as bad as I thought it would be. It never is. Fear is a feeling that is within every one of us. It's what you do when the fear strikes that makes the difference between greatness and mediocrity. There are people that give in, give up and quit. Don't be those people. And remember that you have the control. Free yourself from fear and see yourself grow.

ACTION STEP IV

Describe the last time you got the feeling of fear.
(When, where, what)

_____

_____

_____

_____

_____

_____

_____

_____

_____

In the moments of fear, what have you told yourself?
(Positive or Negative)

_____

_____

_____

_____

_____

_____

_____

_____

_____

Take a deep breath and repeat after me:

I can be successful.
I will be successful.
I am becoming successful.
Repeat this 3 more times

The next time you get the feeling of fear or doubt, I want you to say this to yourself, and then face your fear straight on. Get it done!

In the next chapter, you will learn about goal setting and goal planning to achieve the "impossible".

Step II: Turning Your Happiness into a Jovial Lifestyle

This step is about developing structure and endless happiness in your life.

5

Making it Possible

"When nothing is sure, everything is possible."

MARGARET DRABBLE
ENGLISH NOVELIST,
BIOGRAPHER, & CRITIC

To be jovial is to be full of happiness and joy. It's not just to be happy, because that is temporary. You must be full of happiness to the point where things don't even bother you like they used to. I'll give you an example. Say there's a party this Friday night that you've been excited to go to all week long and it's finally here. You are on your way to this party and all you are thinking about is how much fun you are about to have dancing, chilling and staying out late with your people. When you get there, you realize that there's people standing outside and some are walking away from the location. You then hear from a friend that the party was cancelled, and everyone was told to go home. Now when you're happy, something like this will crush you and change your whole mood. You'll go from being hyped to ready to start a fight. But you see, when you're jovial, your night just started and you'll find another way to make your day. You get your boys or girls together, make some calls, and get the ball rolling. You'll find a different location, a different party or you'll yell out, "who wants pizza?". When you're jovial, it doesn't matter what happens because you are in control. Nothing can bother you.

Before I left college, I made a list of things that I would accomplish within the next couple of years. I wrote that I will get a job that I will love and build it into a career. I will move out of my parents place and into a my own, and I will find a woman that will love me as much as I would love her and start a family. After making the list, I made a promise to myself that when I get that feeling in my chest, when I hear the doubt in my mind, and when I'm in those pivotal moments to make a decision that I will tell myself, "IT IS POSSIBLE", and that I will get it done no matter what. I could not fail, because if things didn't work out the way that I wanted them to, then I would have learned from the experience. Once I was home for the summer after graduation, I was on the go, applying for job after job to work on achieving the goals on my list. I was on the search for a great position with benefits and all. I was not settling for anything small. I wanted what I believed and felt I deserved. Well, things didn't work out for me at first. Each job I applied for was looking for candidates with more experience and they denied me; I couldn't get a break. Then my mom told me about the local YMCA around the block. I had done several summer camps in my day and was done with them at the moment so I fought her on it. In the end, I took that walk to the YMCA and got the job easily as a head sports counselor. I remember attending the summer camp parent meeting and dreading being there. I thought to myself, "I didn't go to school and get my degree for this." I wasn't humble or patient back then as you can tell. Everyone working at the YMCA was either still in college or thinking about going to college & honestly that was not the crowd I wanted to be around after college. Then she walked in and everything slowed down. I immediately stopped thinking about how I felt about the camp and was totally focused on her. She had "IT". And everybody knows that "IT" factor when you see it. I was in total awe. I mean she had the demeanor of a boss. I could tell from the manner in which she carried herself as she entered the room that she was a woman with purpose. She appeared to know who she was &

where she was going. That was that type of company I wanted to be around and learn from. And then I felt it; that feeling in my chest and the sweat in my hands. I told myself just then: "It's Possible". Six years later that woman that walked into the YMCA that night, is now my loving wife, the mother of our beautiful baby girl and most importantly my best friend.

You see the connection? It works in all aspects of life. Whatever it is that you want, you must see it being possible even if you don't believe in it at first. Tell yourself that it will be possible in due time and put in the work in between time. It took me almost 3 years to get to this point with Melissa (my wife). Yes, it was not easy, there was a lot put in to even getting her attention. And if you were to ask her about it today, she'll probably tell you, "Carlos is Crazy and the most persistent person on this planet." And guess what? I still am!

Understand that the universe will move for you like water the moment you decide which way you're going. We really do create our own destiny. Forget that crap about lucky this and lucky that. Lucky happens to those who position themselves to be at the right place at the right time. See it, desire it, and then go get it. It's that simple! And you are going to fail a bunch of times. Some are going to fall harder than others. It's going to happen. What are you going to do about it is the question. I tell my students and players all the time, 20 percent of life is what happens to you, you can't control that, but 80 percent of life is how you react to what happens. The great Les Brown said it best, "If you are going to fall, try to land on your back because if you can at least look up then you can certainly get up." And God knows how many times I've laid there looking up at him asking WHY? Don't quit on your dreams people! Keep pushing towards your goal and believe me when I say it will happen for you! When it gets tough and you want to give up and give in, just close your eyes take a deep breath and tell yourself, "IT'S POSSIBLE."

ACTION STEP V
Describe the life you want 10 years from now. (Work life, home life, family life)

_____

_____

_____

_____

_____

_____

_____

_____

_____

_____

What would it take for you to make this lifestyle possible? List what needs to happen on your end (10-20 things).

_____

_____

_____

_____

_____

_____

_____

_____

_____

_____

In the next chapter, you will learn about the importance of balance and how you can develop balance in
your life.

6

Developing Balance

"Balance is not something you find; it's something you create."

Jana Kingsford
Entrepreneur/Author

I didn't know what was going to happen or how my life would play out after high school. All I knew was that I had to do it well and make those around me proud. The pressure was real, and I felt that I had to do more. So, I got involved and did as much as I could to make myself more qualified for college. I joined more sports teams and clubs, and I participated in more school events to build up my resume while still maintaining my good grades in high school. I tried to keep up, but it all eventually caught up to me. I lost control, and everything began to falter. My grades went down, my performance in my extracurricular activities dipped, and I had less time for everything. I felt I was always in a rush. I was doing too much.

Can you relate? Does this sound familiar to you? It's called "having no balance". Balance is what lays the foundation for you to build and grow from. Balance is what gave me freedom; it's what allowed focus in my life. But what creates balance? It's the prioritizing of importance. You must take the time to think about what is important to you, and write it down.

My wife and I teach at the same school down in Houston. Our drive to work is about 40 – 50 mins there and back home depending on traffic. The ride gives us time to catch up, reflect and talk about our days and or any topic that is relevant to us. A couple of months ago, the topic of balance came up and as we get the rapping on our beliefs and views on it, my wife says the Craziest thing- "Balance is like a Pyramid". At first I was thrown off and confused at what she meant but then she broke it down and enhanced my thinking towards the topic. She explained how balance is all about prioritizing what is important to you. If you make a pyramid and prioritize what's important to you from the peak of the pyramid to the base of pyramid (top to bottom), then you will have balance. Then it hit me and it made sense to me. The pyramid is the structure on which your balance is developed.

So, as my wife told me, "you must see balance as a pyramid". If you put your top 4-5 most important things to you on a pyramid, you will find that the higher you go up the pyramid, the less space there is for anything else. There is no room for distractions at the top of the pyramid. And that is how you must see it- nothing should ever come before what's at the peak of your pyramid.

It was junior year and my basketball team and I had just won the high school basketball Fall Tournament and I was named M.V.P. of the tournament. It was an exciting time. Our hard work was finally paying off and our future as a team looked bright. As we celebrated in the locker room, some of my teammates began to make plans for the night. And then, one of my teammates asked, "We going to egg houses tonight, you coming?". I immediately thought about my priorities and what was most important to me in that moment. And I realized that a risk like that wasn't worth taking if it was going to mess up what I had going for me with school and basketball. So, I told him, "Nah man, I have things to do". The next day, I hear that 5 of my teammates that went that night were caught egging the school principal's house. All 5 teammates were suspended off the team and almost kicked out of school. I could have been in that car but a "fun time" didn't come before school and basketball for me.

I want you to close your eyes and imagine that you could have anything you wanted to have or be anywhere you wanted to be. What would that thing be? Where would you be? Envision it. Feel it. Now write it down. That is what is important to you. Whatever you saw and wrote down is what is most important to you right now. Now you must position yourself to make this dream, or vision, become a reality. How? You start by structuring your pyramid block by block; importance by importance until it's right and it moves you to go for it.

<u>ACTION STEP VI</u>

What are the 4-5 things that are most important to you? List them below.

_____

_____

_____

_____

_____

_____

_____

_____

_____

What are some things that may challenge your pyramid?

_____

_____

_____

_____

_____

_____

_____

_____

_____

_____

Draw your pyramid and put your top 4-5 in it below. What's most important to you (your #1) goes at the top (peek) of your pyramid.

_____

_____

_____

_____

_____

_____

_____

_____

_____

_____

In the next chapter, you will learn about the importance doing things right and finishing what you start.

Step III: Possessing Motivation

This step is about finding and holding on to what inspires you.

7

Do It Right

"If you don't have time to do it right, when will you have time to do it over?"

JOHN WOODEN
AMERICAN BASKETBALL COACH

It happened every weekend on Sunday mornings. It became routine, and there was no hiding from it. Just as the clock would hit 7 A.M., the Salsa music busted through the stereo speakers, and my mom would dance her way into our rooms to wake us all up, one by one. "It's CLEANING DAYYYY!!! Time to get UP! Let's Gooooo!" AHHHH, I hated Sundays. Why was the music so loud? Why did we have to get up so early? And why was she so excited to clean up? I didn't understand. All I knew was that I wanted to get some breakfast, and that's what my mom promised us after we finished cleaning up the whole house every Sunday.

We all had a job to do. My sister would start off by helping my mom clean up all the common areas in the house (living room, kitchen, and bathrooms). My brother and I would start by cutting the grass. I would get the front lawn, and my brother would get the back lawn. After cutting the grass, my brother and I had to help my father clean the cars (inside and out). Then, we all had to clean our rooms. And all of this was usually done by 10 A.M., sometimes 11 A.M. It was exhausting.

I remember trying to clean up as fast as I could. I wanted to beat my siblings. It became a competition, which became more about getting everything done before my siblings rather than cleaning to the best of my abilities. This got me in trouble. My parents never let me cut corners and take the easy route. But I would still try. My father would always make me clean the car over again if I didn't clean it properly the first time. My mother would always make me re-clean my room if it wasn't dusted right. She would tell me "You need to dust under things not just around things". I just wanted to finish! But then I began to realize that I was taking more time by "rushing." My parents would check if things were done right, and if they weren't, I was told to clean it again. So, at the end of the day, I was actually doing more work. This is when I made the decision to work smarter, not faster.

In the heat of the moment, we tend to all focus on just getting things done, and sometimes we miss opportunities because we don't do things the right way the first time around. We all must be motivated to get things right in the moment. It's about giving your all and working on your ability to focus in the moment. No matter what it is, you must own it!

ACTION STEP VII

What have you cut corners on? And what were your reasons for taking the easy route each time? List below.

_____

_____

_____

_____

_____

_____

_____

_____

_____

What will make you do it right the first time? What will you think about in those moments?

_____

_____

_____

_____

_____

_____

_____

_____

_____

In the next chapter, you will learn about the power of presence and the importance of control.

8

What Lion Are You?

"The truth is like a lion. You don't have to defend it. Let it loose. It will defend itself."

St. Augustine
Christian Theologian and
Philosopher

I remember vividly seeing the pain in my mother's eyes. She didn't have to say much. It was all in her body language and in her face. My mother dealt with a lot of crap from my pops growing up, but this time, he had crossed the line and went too far. I was little and wasn't supposed to comprehend what was going on, but I did. My mom noticed, and grab me by the face, looked me in the eyes and said "Don't EVER treat women like that, you hear me! Be better than that!" I think about those exact words every time I interact with my wife, my daughter or any woman that crosses my path.

I want you to take a second and seriously think about what makes a man a man to you. What are the qualities that make someone a man? Think about an experience that you had in your life that made you believe in what you think a man is. Was it a movie you saw? T.V. show you watched? Song you heard? A person you seen? You see, I think most males don't know why they treat women the way that they do. I believe they have just been doing what they thought men are supposed to do from what they were exposed to. You must understand that there is a difference between how you **think** you should react and how you **want** to react. A boy becomes a man when he becomes who he wants to become regardless of what people may think. Are you doing what you want or what you think is cool to do?

I was raised to believe that a man is someone that is supposed to provide security and protection to a woman, not fear. Yes, we have aggression inside us, but you must learn to channel that aggression towards the right things. I channel my aggression towards protecting women. I turn into a beast when I see a woman in harm's way, it comes natural to me. I can't see a woman be disrespected by a man. It bothers me to my core and reminds me of the pain I saw my mom go through when I was growing up.

It's like the lion mentality. Have you ever seen a lion fight? They are straight savages when it comes to protecting their own. People think lions just attack for no reason, but if you pay close attention, you will see that they never attack the weak or the young. They don't waste their time with that. They know that they can do damage to those who are smaller, weaker, or younger. Their presence alone lets others know who the king of the jungle is. They channel and focus their aggression on the beast that threatens their domain, their kingdom. Most boys think they are the lion taking down the beast when they yell at and disrespect women, but they're not. They look weak when they do that. They are the lion attacking the cub when they do that. Understand that a man's presence alone should be enough. Our voices have base for a reason; we don't need to yell. True strength is control. Which lion do you want to be?

ACTION STEP VIII
List all the men that were a part of your life below.
(Could be family members, friend, mentors, or celebrities you followed)

_____

_____

_____

_____

_____

_____

_____

_____

_____

Which one of these men had the greatest influence on you and why?

_____

_____

_____

_____

_____

_____

_____

_____

_____

_____

Question to my male readers:
What kind of man do you want to be?

_____

_____

_____

_____

_____

_____

_____

_____

_____

_____

Question to my female readers:
What kind of men do you want around in your life?

_____

_____

_____

_____

_____

_____

_____

_____

_____

_____

In the next chapter, you will learn about the importance of acting on your dreams as soon as possible.

9

When is Now Good for You?

"If we wait until we're ready, we'll be waiting for the rest of our lives."

LEMONY SNICKET
AMERICAN NOVELIST

I ask my students all the time "What do you want to be when you get older?" They tell me "I want to be a doctor Mr. M; a teacher, a soccer player, a basketball player; Mr. M I want to be an actor." My initial thought after they tell me their goals is, great! They know what they want. Then I ask them, "WHEN? When is "NOW" a good time? When is "NOW" a good time for you to start working on that goal you want to achieve; for you to start becoming that person you want to become?" You see, we all want something out of life whether you admit it or not. We think about what we want, tell ourselves and others about what we want, and then we have been conditioned to wait, telling ourselves we have time, we're young, it'll happen. This idea of time is what is holding us back from achieving anything. It doesn't just happen. Success is NOT an accident. Those who have achieve already knew what they wanted and acted on it. You are wasting time waiting. If you want to be a better person, a better athlete, a better student, son, daughter, brother, sister, even a better partner to someone, you must start working on becoming that now or else you will always be talking about later. When you want to be successful, there is no "later". There's NOW and Only NOW.

Taking the first step was the hardest thing for me to do. I fear to fail, or hurt, again. But you see, I had to learn how to use what happened to me to my advantage. A wise person by the name of Les Brown once said, "The tougher the battle, the sweater the victory. The harder it is, the stronger you will become." We are all going to go through difficult times. You must own your struggle. Own your pain. I have a tattoo on my right arm that reads, "My Pain is My Motivation." I used the pain early in my life to mold me into what and who I am today. You have the power to decide if your pain is going to break you or make you. I took what I saw and had around me and used it as my motivation. You have the power to do that. I saw my father almost drink his life away. I saw the pain my father caused my mother. I witnessed my father attempt suicide, twice. Then I was there when my mother and father broke down in my arms because a close family member, too, attempted suicide. I love my family, but there were some things that I witnessed growing up that I did not want for myself. I saw what I could become if I were not to control my life. I don't blame my pain anymore; I'm thankful for my pain. My parents did the best they could, but I saw better for myself. I had to do different and change the course. It made no sense for me to do the same. I wasn't going to make it my excuse. I flipped my script. You have the power to flip your script, if it's not what you see for yourself. You see there's two types of people in this world- the person who wakes up, looks out the window and sees the beautiful sunrise and then there's that person that wakes up, looks at the window, and focuses on the fog on that window. You must look through your fog and see your sunrise. It's going to be hard, beyond challenging, and painful at times, and if you haven't experienced struggle yet, it's coming. But if you learn from what happens to you and you use it to your advantage, then you too can stand stronger than ever before because you didn't let it break you! Nothing can stop you!

Listen to yourself. Tell yourself you are GREAT until you convince yourself and BELIEVE you are. If you take this mentally, then you will start acting and behaving like you are great. Desire better than what is presented to you. That feeling will then drive you to act and move towards where you want to be. Stop waiting for more time, it will past. Walk where there is no path, and leave a trail.

ACTION STEP IX

What do you want to accomplish now? List 2-4 of the goals you are looking to accomplish within the next couple of months and or year.

_____

_____

_____

_____

_____

_____

_____

_____

_____

_____

What actions are to taking daily to make these goals come true?

_____

_____

_____

_____

_____

_____

_____

_____

_____

_____

In the next chapter, you will learn about the importance of effort and how it can change your life.

10

Let Your Effort Show

"Your best will never be ignored."

CARLOS J. MALAVE
EDUCATOR/MOTIVATIONAL SPEAKER/
AUTHOR

When I was six years old, I told my father to shave the hair off my head so that I could look like Michael Jordan. He laughed, as he asked why. Serious as can be, I looked him in the eye and said, "To be the BEST, you have to look like the BEST. And I want to be the BEST". After two hours of persuading, my father finally gave in, and I was granted my first bald head.

The first goal that I ever had growing up was to become a basketball player. It's all I wanted and needed at one point in my life. The game brought me so much joy, and for a few hours a day, it became my escape from the world. I loved to play, watch, and talk about the game as much as I could. But I quickly learned that just because I loved and knew everything about the game, it didn't mean that I would automatically be great at it. The truth was I SUCKED!

It took me some time to admit it, but I couldn't deny how bad I was out on the basketball court. Although I could handle the ball well, I wasn't any good at passing or shooting the ball. This made me a huge liability on the basketball court, and everyone let me know about it.

It was the last game of the year for the junior varsity team, and I had just played the worst game I have ever played in my entire life. We were embarrassed by our opponent, and the best player on the other team made me look like a fool in front of the whole school. The crowd booed us, and I even heard people chanting, "You Suck" as we walked off the court. I remember sitting in the locker room, all by myself, after everyone had left, and breaking down into tears. It was the first time I had ever cried after a game. I was destroyed, broken down and hurt but I knew that I had to make a change.

When I got home that night, I sat in my room and reflected for hours. I wanted to figure out why I was so hurt and bothered by what happened. I concluded that I wasn't upset because I played bad; I was upset because I didn't give my best. A part of me knew that I could have given more of me throughout the game. I got into my own head, and I didn't push myself. Before I went to bed that night, I looked myself in the mirror and said, "This will never happen again. I will give my all to the game from this day forward."

The first thing I did was adjust my daily practice regiment. I wanted to be more prepared and in shape than everyone else, and to do so, I had to start doing what I knew my friends and teammates weren't. I decided I had to get up earlier and practice more often. So, for the rest of the school year, I got up every morning before school and shot over 500 jump shots. When I got home from school I would shoot another 500 jump shots. It was extremely hard and I struggled to get it done at times but I stuck with it and made it my routine. When the summer came, everything was intensified, and the workouts were multiplied. My summer routine changed. Every morning, I would wake up and shoot 1,000 jump shots before the sun came up, then go inside, shower, eat and watch old game tape of Michael Jordan, Magic Johnson, or Larry Bird. In the afternoon, I would run 3 miles to the local park and shoot another 1,000 jump shots before everyone came down to play. Then I would play with everyone and when everyone left, I would stay and shoot another 1,000 shots. I did this every day. Then one day Coach Powell, the JV coach, joined me as I was shooting my usual 1,000 shots before everyone arrived. He told me that he had been watching me over the last couple of months and noticed my hard work. He was impressed and wanted to help. So, he began to train me. Every evening, after I would do my daily practice regiments in the mornings and afternoons, I would meet him at the park at 4 p.m. and we would train. The following year I became an All- Conference Player and the MVP of the School's Varsity Basketball team.

My effort didn't go unnoticed; your effort won't go unnoticed. Work like hell for what you want and the help will come. If you give your all to what you want, you will never be overlooked by anyone. It might not happen as quickly as you may like it, but you must trust in the process. The process will always lead you towards your progress.

ACTION STEP X

List all the people that have helped you along the way. (teachers, coaches, friends, mentors, etc.)

_____

_____

_____

_____

_____

_____

_____

_____

_____

Did you ask for their help each time? Why or why not?

_____

_____

_____

_____

_____

_____

_____

_____

_____

Have your efforts been acknowledged? Are you giving your all to what you want? Explain.

_____

_____

_____

_____

_____

_____

_____

_____

_____

_____

Conclusion: You Can Do It!

"Become conscious, jovial and motivated through your own experiences to achieve evolution in your life."

CARLOS J. MALAVE
EDUCATOR/MOTIVATIONAL SPEAKER/
AUTHOR

A high school teacher once told me, "There are no greater lessons than the ones that life will teach you." Over time, I've come to realize that life is the greatest educator of them all. Life has given me the knowledge, awareness, and motivation that still drives me today. It is the experiences of life that make us who we are. And I'm telling you that if you use and perceive your experiences wisely, then you too can have the success you dream of.

I believe that we were all blessed with something special. We have been given definite talents and skills in which we can all access. I am certain that we have been put onto our specific paths in life to find and nourish these gifts. We were made for the circumstances we were born into. You must use what you were given and maximize it to reach your full potential. Don't blame the process rather claim your progress and enhance your life.

A year ago, I took the initials to my name (C.J.M) and I created my brand, Conscious Jovial Motivation. I became conscious of what was happening around me. I took my experiences and use them to create a jovial lifestyle. I continue to stay motivated by what I could become throughout the process. You can become conscious, jovial, and motivated to create and build your future. Trust yourself and work as if today's effort will lead you to tomorrow's glory.

Final Thoughts

You read, you answered questions and you reflected on your own experiences. Now what do you do? Where do you go from here? Well, the next step is to act. It's time to apply what you've learned in this book to your own life. I want you to view this book as your starting point towards success. Use it as a guide to achieve your goals. We worked on some big things throughout this book together. I want you to take some time and look over your reflections in each chapter. You can start anywhere you would like. Choose your favorite chapters and review what you wrote down at the end of those chapters, then I want you to accept the challenge and act. Do something that you wrote down; something that you know needs to be done now. Every act you take won't be easy to do but remember that the first act is always the toughest. Just start and I promise you, it will get easier and you will get better. You came this far. Don't turn back now. There are people that talk about becoming better individuals and there are people that work on becoming better individuals. Work! I believe in you! Good luck!

Acknowledgments

If I acknowledge all the people who have had a helping hand in getting me to this point in my life where I'm able to write about success, we might be here forever and this book will never end. Let me just sum it up by saying that I want to thank everyone who has had any hand in any measure of the success that I have accomplished- you know who you are, and I want to thank you all.

I want to thank the two master teachers at Yes Prep Gulfton, Meghan Holmes and Crystal Visperas. These two wonderful women took time out of their very busy schedules to edit my work. This book would not be what it is without their efforts. You made this book possible and I appreciate you both. Thank you!

I would also like to thank all the students that I have taught and coached throughout the years. This book was written with you guys in mind. "Translating Your Success" was inspired by all the students at both Inwood Academy for Leadership Charter School in New York City and Yes Prep Public School at Gulfton in Houston Texas.

To each one of my past students at Inwood Academy for Leadership Charter School, thank you. You challenged me, you pushed me but most importantly, you made me better as a leader of people. I wouldn't be the educator I am today if it weren't for my experience at Inwood Academy. You will always be close to my heart Inwood. Love you guys!

To all my current and future students at Yes Prep Gulfton, I thank you. You accepted me for my differences and showed me a new world out here in Texas. We laughed together, we cried together and we grew together over the last couple of years. You showed me how to connect and relate to the youth better. You all became conscious thinkers in my eyes during my classes while I became a motivator and now author in your eyes. Thank you for believing in me and supporting me. All I wanted to be was an example for you. Now it's time for you to do you and achieve your goals. I'm excited to see what you guys do in the future.

About the Author

Carlos J. Malave has many years of experience coaching and inspiring young people. He taught health and physical education for five years in the New York City area and in Houston. He has also served as a coach, including high school girls' basketball, middle school flag foot-  ball, middle school soccer, and middle school track and field. In addition to working as a physical trainer and a life coach, he has served as a public speaker for youth programs, community centers, and college events.

"My purpose is to help people Consciously use their experiences to create a Jovial & Motivated lifestyle."

Recommendations

<u>Kyle Vidrine</u>

- Speaker/ Author & Co- Founder of PEN

"After reading about Carlos's life and everything that he has been through, he's truly the definition of being resilient. A lot of speakers speak about motivation and inspiration from a book's viewpoint, but Carlos speaks from his heart and his own personal experiences about overcoming and push through life's trials. I look for and expect him to do amazing things in the future."

<u>Jamie Paperato</u>

- Co- Founder & CEO at JPHigherED

"It is with great pleasure that I recommend Carlos J. Malave to any organization, school, or business in need of a motivational speaker. Over the past seven years, I have had the opportunity to witness Carlos' dedication to serving others through compassion and truth-telling. Carlos' unique experiences, deep reflection, and brilliant insights make him an asset to any organization."

Ezra P. Scott Jr.

- Niagara Fall City Councilman

"The trouble wasn't finding or choosing the skill but rather believing in one."

"I am excited to see Carlos pursuing this gift and passion that he has. Motivating and inspiring comes naturally for Carlos. He was not only my point guard (floor general) in college. But I remember meeting Carlos in my early weeks of transferring to SUNY Cortland. Carlos lit a fire under me to train and condition hard allowing me to make the Men's Varsity Basketball team. That same motivation and work ethic follows me today. Thank you for all that you do, Carlos!!!"

Noelle Chaddock Paley

- Associate Dean of Diversity and Inclusion in Academic Affairs at Rhodes College

"Mr. Malave is the consummate success story. As a keynote and life coach, Mr. Malave invokes self-reflection and a commitment to the greater good. Mr. Malave makes us all want to try harder. Bringing Mr. Malave into your event or workshop as a keynote is to assure your participants and guests leaving with renewed spirit and conviction. Mr. Malave speaks truth to power and calls us all to dig deep and do better. Having known Mr. Malave as a rough and tumble kid from NYC, I can attest to his evolution as a professional, coach, teacher, and engaged world citizen. Mr. Malave is brilliant, poignant, and absolutely the funniest person I know. Choose Malave today. You will move the lives you serve that much closer to greatness."

Erik J. Bitterbaum

- President at State University of New York at Cortland

"Carlos was a dedicated physical education student who involved himself as an undergraduate in professional organizations in his field including the New York State Association for Health, Physical Education, Recreation and Dance (NYSAHPERD), the American Alliance for Health, Physical Education, Recreation and Dance (AAHPERD), and the SUNY Cortland Alliance of Physical Education Majors (APEM).

In addition to academics, Carlos served as a resident assistant for one year, and he was an active participant in extracurricular activities, including serving as president of the Caribbean Student Association (CSA) on campus in 2010. His contributions to the campus community were recognized with several awards, including the SUNY Cortland Leadership Award for (Fall 2009 Leadership Retreat), the Leadership Award for Student Keynote Speaker at 1st SUNY Cortland Diversity Conference, Spring 2010, the National Residence Hall Honorary for SUNY Cortland "Of the Month Award" for outstanding contributions as a Spotlight Resident Assistant, January 2011, and the National Residence Hall Honorary for SUNY

Cortland "Of the Month Award" for An Outstanding Educational Program, February 2011.

Carlos was an asset to the student body at SUNY Cortland. He exemplifies the spirit we wish to instill in our students and alumni – he has gone into the world and is positively changing the lives of others. I recommend Carlos Malave to you without reservation."

Christopher A. Diaz

- Student Support Counselor at YES Prep Gulfton

"Mr. Malave is a passionate educator from New York that provides us with a wondrous perspective of the world. I remember when I first walked into his classroom; he was instructing on goal setting. He provided a personal example related to how it has always been a goal of his to have a home with a yard and upon relocating to Texas he saw to making that dream a reality. His delivery was riveting. The story was captivating and inspirational. Carlos is a very well-spoken man; articulate & conscious. I cannot recollect the last time I became so enraptured by a classroom lecture or lesson. Often times, I find myself remaining in his classroom despite needing to attend to matters elsewhere if for nothing more than to simply overhear a few more minutes of his teachings. It is not solely his tone or pace, but his disposition that lends itself to his ability to command an audience. And more importantly, it is the humility he exudes as he goes about accomplishing his works that I respect most of all."

<u>Tara Lee Vaughn</u>

- Health Education Specialist

"Carlos has motivational speaking skills where he can speak to teens in a way that they genuinely understand. While Carlos has a great natural aptitude for public speaking, he also works diligently to hone his craft. Carlos is a joy to work with because he has the type of attitude that is optimistic in a very encouraging way. Carlos sees the potential in everyone around him and I hope to work with him again soon."